First published in 2014 by
Clarity Media Ltd
www.clarity-media.co.uk

Puzzles created by Dan Moore
Design and layout by Amy Smith

About Clarity Media

Clarity Media are a leading provider of a huge range of puzzles for adults and children. For more information on our services, please visit us at www.pzle.co.uk. For information on purchasing puzzles for publication, visit us at www.clarity-media.co.uk

Puzzle Magazines

If you enjoy the puzzles in this book, then you may be interested in our puzzle magazines. We have a very large range of magazines that you can download and print yourself in PDF format at our Puzzle Magazine site. For more information, take a look
at http://www.puzzle-magazine.com

Online Puzzles

If you prefer to play puzzles online, please take a look at the Puzzle Club website, at
www.thepuzzleclub.com

We also have more puzzle books available at
www.puzzle-book.co.uk

Contents:

Half-Alpha Crossword

In these crosswords all your answers must only contain letters from the first half of the alphabet, as listed underneath each puzzle. The letters N – Z must not appear in a single one of your answers!

Jigsaw Crossword

The solution grid has been split into small pieces. You must work out where each piece goes in the grid to solve the puzzle and reveal the completed crossword grid. Each piece is used exactly once. The clues are given to help you solve the puzzle.

Ladder Crossword

Can you fill the letter ladder by solving all the standard crossword clues?

Just The Once Crossword

There are 26 clues in this crossword variant, and the answers start with each of the letters A – Z exactly once. So if you place the word 'Example' as one of your answers, no other answer can start with the letter 'E', and so on. The across and down clues for the puzzle are given, but in random order, so you'll need to work out where each answer fits in the grid to solve the puzzle.

Word Square

Word squares are mini 4 x 4 crossword puzzles with a fun twist – the answers are the same in both the across and down direction!

Pangram Crossword

A pangram is a standard crossword puzzle, but it must contain each letter from A – Z one or more times. A cross-out letter grid is given underneath the puzzle so you can record which letters you've used.

Star Letter Crossword

These are ordinary crossword puzzles but with a twist: each puzzle has a 'star letter' that must appear at least once in every single one of your answers. The star letter is given at the start of each puzzle.

Triplet Crossword

In these puzzles all answers must start with one of three letters that are given at the top of each puzzle. For instance, if the puzzle is 'ABC Triplet' then all answers must start with either A, B or C.

Anagram Crossword

All the clues in these puzzles are anagrams of the answers: sometimes there will be more than one possible anagram of a series of letters so you'll need to cross-reference other answers in the grid to find the correct anagram to fill the grid.

A-Z Puzzles

Each letter of the alphabet from A – Z has been removed from the grid once, to leave 26 empty circled squares. You must work out which letter from A – Z fits in each of the blank circles and write it in, so as to fill the crossword grid and solve the puzzle.

Double Definition

A double definition crossword is a standard crossword puzzle, but each clue contains not one but two definitions for each answer word.

Every Letter Counts

In these mini-crosswords you are given a list of letters that each appear just once in the grid. You must solve the crossword clues using each letter from the list a single time – every letter really does count!

Skeleton Crossword

With a skeleton crossword you not only need to solve the clues to fill the grid but also build the grid at the same time. Each grid exhibits standard 180 degree rotational symmetry. Some starter numbers and blank cells are given to get you started. Use this information along with the clues and the grid symmetry to solve the puzzle and complete the grid. Good luck!

Spiral Crossword

In a spiral crossword you start at the top left and work your way clockwise around the grid until you reach the central square. The last letter of an answer is shared with the first letter of the next answer. Two other words will appear in the grey diagonals once the grid is complete.

Vowelless Crossword

The clues for vowelless crosswords are the answer words – but without any of their vowels! For instance the clue 'FT' could be answered with 'FAT' or 'FIT'. You'll need to use your vocabulary and knowledge of the English language to work out the possible words that can fit each letter pattern, together with the other answers in the grid to work out which option must be placed where there is more than one possible matching word.

Good Luck &
Happy Solving!

Across

1 - Country in southern Asia (5)

4 - Person of high rank (7)

7 - Wander off track (5)

8 - Group of spectators (8)

9 - Equipped (5)

11 - Parroted (anag) (8)

15 - And so on (2,6)

17 - Gain knowledge (5)

19 - Hindered (8)

20 - Make a sound expressing pain (5)

21 - Characteristics (7)

22 - Chopping (5)

Down

1 - Fair (9)

2 - Deliberately impassive (7)

3 - Is present at (7)

4 - South American cowboy (6)

5 - Character of a person (6)

6 - Fill with high spirits (5)

10 - Requiring much skill (of a task) (9)

12 - Part of the ocean (4,3)

13 - Italian fast racing car (7)

14 - Refined in manner (6)

16 - Short written works (6)

18 - British noblemen (5)

Across

7 - Money lent to publicly acknowledge (6)

8 - Snooker ball shade (6)

10 - Drug unlikely to cause offence (7)

11 - Furniture to put a motion forward (5)

12 - Program cipher (4)

13 - Comic party (5)

17 - Ornament to delight greatly (5)

18 - Trotter to pay the bill (4)

22 - Discard rubbish (5)

23 - One with innate talent, not synthetic (7)

24 - Reprimand to increase rapidly (6)

25 - Expert prophet (6)

Down

1 - Cancel score (7)

2 - Backs brief moments (7)

3 - Plastic record (5)

4 - Happy innards (7)

5 - Idiot bird (5)

6 - Command organisation (5)

9 - Foreign or outlandish falcon (9)

14 - Axe helicopter (7)

15 - Counteract right (7)

16 - Stopped running and ceased making progress (7)

19 - Operators - those who exploit others (5)

20 - Stunt fool (5)

21 - Begin twitch (5)

The crossword grid with numbered cells (1-25) and letter columns A through Z below.

A B C D E F G H I J K L M N O P Q R S T U V W X Y Z

Across

1 - Rounded mass of steamed dough (8)

6 - Consumes (4)

8 - Willow twigs (6)

9 - Keyboard instruments (6)

10 - In what way (3)

11 - True information (4)

12 - Ten more than eighty (6)

13 - Reformulate (6)

15 - Utterly senseless (6)

17 - Lizard (6)

20 - Joke (4)

21 - Bleat of a sheep (3)

22 - Structures or models (6)

23 - The flowing back of a liquid (6)

24 - Sleepy (4)

25 - Stocky (8)

Down

2 - Upmarket (7)

3 - Crimp (5)

4 - Towards the coast (7)

5 - Adult (5)

6 - Motors (7)

7 - Religious doctrine (5)

14 - Idiotically (7)

15 - Fish tanks (7)

16 - Ecstatic joy (7)

18 - Lizard (5)

19 - Embarrass (5)

20 - Short time (5)

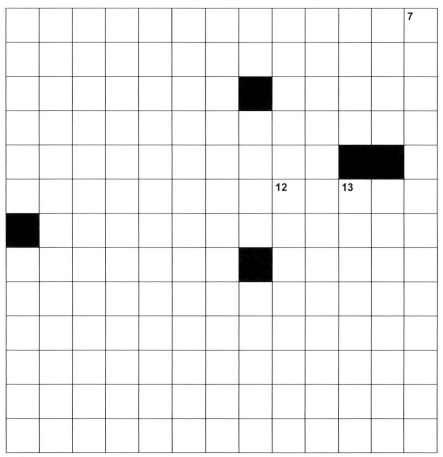

Across

1 - Eg Iceland

4 - Norway lobsters

9 - Inactive pill

10 - Open-meshed material

11 - Makes musical sounds

12 - Parts in a play

14 - Wound the pride of

15 - Cylinder of smoking tobacco

17 - Go inside

18 - Natural environment

20 - Measure of how pressing something is

21 - Patterns

22 - Ranked based on merit

Down

1 - Enforce compliance with

2 - Discovering; finding out

3 - Requirements

5 - Apprehend; snare

6 - The south of France

7 - Pictures

8 - An argument that does not follow

13 - Heard

14 - Imaginary

15 - Roman military unit

16 - Made a victim of

17 - Keen

19 - Computer memory unit

A B C D E F G H I J K L M N O P Q R S T U V W X Y Z

Across

1 - RJNDR

8 - TMPRTR

9 - NTTL

11 - FR

13 - XD

14 - RNWS

16 - DSTRCTV

18 - NBNDD

Down

2 - LM

3 - PNLY

4 - NR

5 - MLT

6 - STNDRDS

7 - DPRSSD

10 - TRSN

12 - DCN

15 - TR

17 - R

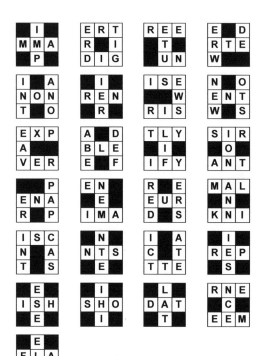

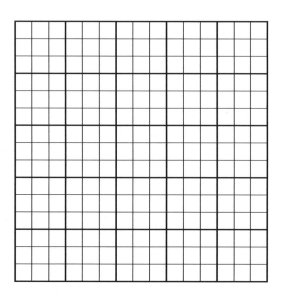

Can you slot the jigsaw pieces into the grid correctly, to create a completed crossword? Use the clues we have listed below to help you out. The grid exhibits standard crossword grid symmetry.

Across

1 - Country where one finds Bamako (4)

9 - Not catching fire easily (3-9)

10 - Make a garment using wool (4)

11 - Circumspectly (10)

15 - Lessen (7)

16 - Bring together (5)

18 - Skill (9)

19 - Statistics and facts (4)

20 - Express a desire for (4)

21 - Green patina formed on copper (9)

23 - Warning noise from an emergency vehicle (5)

24 - People who rent property (7)

26 - Eg positrons (10)

29 - Sea eagle (4)

30 - Someone who sets up their own business (12)

31 - Appear to be (4)

Down

2 - Total destruction (12)

3 - Entwine (10)

4 - Positive electrode (5)

5 - Trees of the genus Ulmus (4)

6 - Momentum (7)

7 - Encourage in wrongdoing (4)

8 - Openly refuse to obey an order (4)

12 - Forbid (9)

13 - Reprimand severely (9)

14 - Jail term without end (4,8)

17 - Daily periodicals (10)

22 - Foes (7)

25 - Made a mistake (5)

26 - Once more (4)

27 - Small children (4)

28 - Row or level of a structure (4)

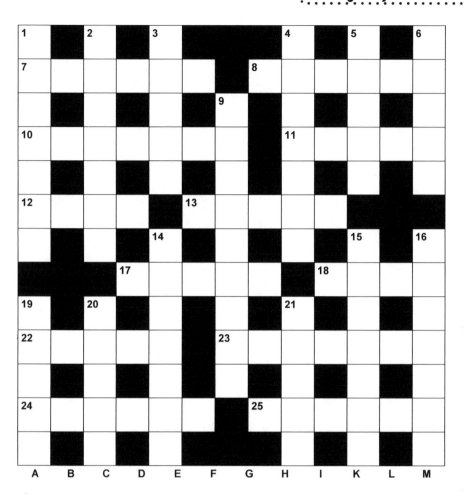

Across

7 - Frozen water spear (6)

8 - Packed (6)

10 - Brazilian dance (7)

11 - ___ Izzard: stand-up comedian (5)

12 - Every (4)

13 - Third Greek letter (5)

17 - In front (5)

18 - Bivalve marine mollusc (4)

22 - Sweet-scented shrub (5)

23 - Forbidden by law (7)

24 - Moved at an easy pace (6)

25 - Stout-bodied insect (6)

Down

1 - Dealt with a tough question (7)

2 - Novelty (7)

3 - Epic poem ascribed to Homer (5)

4 - Difficult choice (7)

5 - Edge of a knife (5)

6 - Summed together (5)

9 - Tree known for the nut it produces (9)

14 - Verified (7)

15 - Mournful (7)

16 - Mercury alloy (7)

19 - Simple aquatic plants (5)

20 - Church farmland (5)

21 - Threshing tool (5)

9 Every Letter Counts

Across

1 - ___ in: eat heartily (4)

3 - Hogs (4)

Down

1 - Confine; snare (4)

2 - Items that unlock doors (4)

A C E G I K
P R S T U Y

10 Ladder Crossword

Across

3 - Impel; spur on (4)

4 - Mongrel dog (4)

5 - Robert De ___ : actor (4)

6 - Adolescent (abbrev) (4)

7 - ___ Sharif: Egyptian actor (4)

Down

1 - Highest point (11)

2 - Region including Cornwall and Devon (4,7)

Across

7 - On a ship or train (6)

8 - Subsidiary action (6)

10 - Light beard (7)

11 - ___ gas: eg neon or argon (5)

12 - Comply (4)

13 - Pierces (5)

17 - Facial hair (5)

18 - Robe (anag) (4)

22 - Seventh sign of the zodiac (5)

23 - Slanting (7)

24 - Insect of the order Coleoptera (6)

25 - Physical item (6)

Down

1 - Double-reed instrument (7)

2 - Payments in addition to wages (7)

3 - Babies' beds (5)

4 - Eventually (2,3,2)

5 - Church farmland (5)

6 - Computer memory units (5)

9 - Mail slot (6,3)

14 - Plausible; defensible (7)

15 - Bunch of flowers (7)

16 - Below (7)

19 - Bludgeons (5)

20 - Henrik ___ : Norwegian author (5)

21 - Excuse of any kind (5)

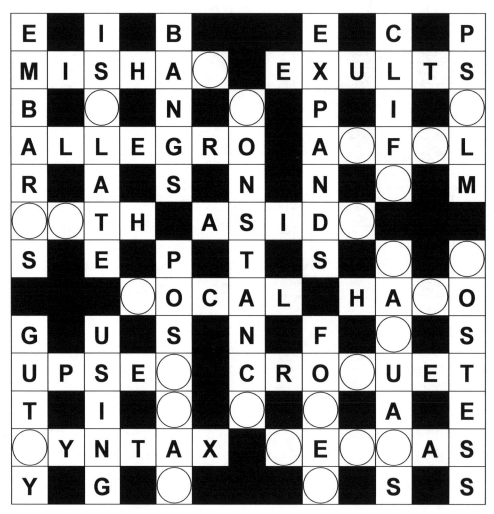

A B C D E F G H I J K L M N O P Q R S T U V W X Y Z

A B C D E F G H I J K L M N O P Q R S T U V W X Y Z

Across

7 - Continent (6)

8 - Conclude (6)

10 - Confine (7)

11 - Angry (5)

12 - Chopped (4)

13 - Acknowledged; assumed (5)

17 - Additional payment for good performance (5)

18 - Tool (4)

22 - Forelock of hair (5)

23 - Page templates (7)

24 - Urges to act (6)

25 - Side to side movement (6)

Down

1 - Polish (7)

2 - More important (7)

3 - Prickly (5)

4 - Says out loud (7)

5 - Pertaining to the moon (5)

6 - Hand tool (5)

9 - Gravely (9)

14 - Light fluffy dish (7)

15 - Declare to be (7)

16 - Restrained (7)

19 - Furnish or supply (5)

20 - Slips (anag) (5)

21 - Verse form (5)

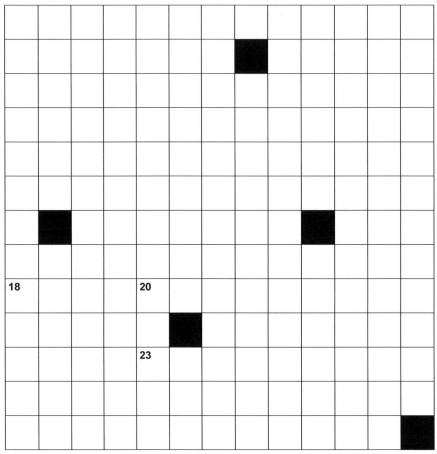

Across

1 - Very busy and full

9 - Became less intense

10 - Level golf score

11 - Aimed (anag)

12 - ___ Dushku: US actress

13 - Disregards

16 - Approximate

18 - Opposite of lows

21 - Suffuse with colour

22 - Part of a pen

23 - Undo a knot

24 - Sent back to one's own country

Down

2 - Sausages in bread rolls

3 - Declare (anag)

4 - Support; help

5 - Shelf

6 - Island in the Bay of Naples

7 - Becoming less

8 - Rent manager (anag)

14 - Mediterranean resort area

15 - Cab ride (anag)

17 - Stationary part of a motor

19 - Triangular wall part

20 - Small room used as a steam bath

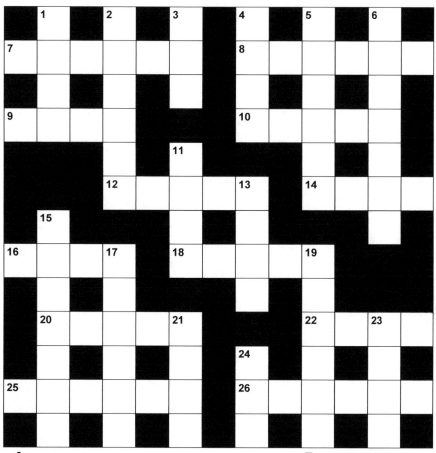

Across

A fact that has been verified (5)

A ball game (5)

Series of linked metal rings (5)

Ox-like mammals (4)

Striped animal (5)

Remove goods from a van (6)

Cry of derision (4)

Wild horse (6)

___ Moore: Hollywood actress (4)

Ancient Persian king (6)

Utilise wrongly (6)

Catch sight of (4)

Down

Sharp chopping implement (3)

Risky undertaking (7)

Smiles contemptuously (6)

Alumnus of a public school (3,3)

Child who has no home (4)

Area of a church (4)

Platform leading out to sea (4)

Large lizard (6)

Ask questions (4)

Come together (3)

Set of instructions (6)

Foot of a horse (4)

Caustic calcium compound (4)

Form of singing for entertainment (7)

Across

7 - Seek to hurt (6)

8 - Next to (6)

10 - United States (7)

11 - ___ Adkins: singer (5)

12 - Mountain system in Europe (4)

13 - Starting point (5)

17 - Obscure road (5)

18 - Bay (4)

22 - Excuse of any kind (5)

23 - Upset; affect (7)

24 - Item of neckwear (6)

25 - Evoke a feeling (6)

Down

1 - Yellow fruits (7)

2 - Try (7)

3 - Bitterly pungent (5)

4 - Made of clay hardened by heat (7)

5 - Alcoholic beverage (5)

6 - Beets (anag) (5)

9 - Boat (9)

14 - Sceptical (7)

15 - Abundant (7)

16 - Insects with biting mouthparts (7)

19 - Group of goods produced at one time (5)

20 - Cylinder of smoking tobacco (5)

21 - Burning (5)

Across

1 - PAARCACE

6 - THTIG

7 - TIRSP

9 - ERWE

10 - LKTREI

12 - ANYMAL

14 - WKSE

17 - ABSAM

18 - GNOLA

19 - TOSEISNI

Down

2 - LGEAA

3 - CSTA

4 - ASSLAI

5 - GTEER

6 - TSLREIL

8 - RGPWEII

11 - AIASFR

13 - ENYEM

15 - NTKSO

16 - LMIA

18 Spiral Crossword

The last letter of each answer will become the first letter of the next answer.
Two other words will appear in the grey diagonals.

1 - With hands on the hips
2 - Sets of six balls (cricket)
3 - Poor handwriting
4 - Relay (anag)
5 - Exposes to danger
6 - Reigns (anag)
7 - Appreciates
8 - Majestic
9 - Children
10 - Lure
11 - Amended
12 - Danes (anag)
13 - Thick drink
14 - Background actors
15 - Grain store
16 - Upon

19 Word Square

Aromatic herb

Suggestion

Tax

Puts down

Across

1 - Male monarch (4)

3 - Send down a ball in cricket (4)

Down

1 - Pavement edge (4)

2 - Ancient France (4)

A B E G I K
L N O R U W

Across

3 - Abominable snowman (4)

4 - Circular storage medium (4)

5 - Domestic cattle (4)

6 - Hired form of transport (4)

7 - Unwrap (4)

Down

1 - Act of publishing content in several places (11)

2 - Debates (11)

Across

1 - Unit of linear measure (4)

3 - Explicit and clearly stated (8)

9 - Former Greek monetary unit (7)

10 - Capital of Ghana (5)

11 - Go away from quickly (5)

12 - Bodies of writing (7)

13 - Pull back from (6)

15 - Form-fitting garment (6)

17 - Emotional stability (7)

18 - Performer (5)

20 - Cluster (5)

21 - Fragrant compound (7)

22 - Overshadows (8)

23 - Great tennis serves (4)

Down

1 - Incapable of being expressed in words (13)

2 - Lead a discussion (5)

4 - Flatfish (6)

5 - Ability to see the future (12)

6 - Influences that contribute to a result (7)

7 - Dull and uninteresting (13)

8 - Type of contest (12)

14 - Army rank (7)

16 - Determine (6)

19 - Uniform jacket (5)

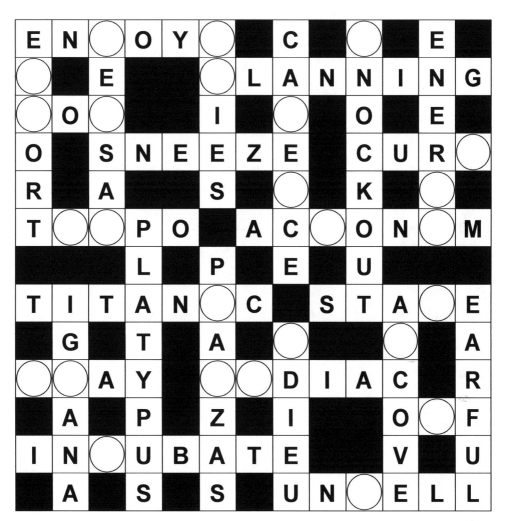

A B C D E F G H I J K L M N O P Q R S T U V W X Y Z

Across

1 - Mexican cloak (6)

7 - Liable to error (8)

8 - Knock vigorously (3)

9 - Common bird (6)

10 - Relocate (4)

11 - Marsh plant (5)

13 - Act of putting pen to paper (7)

15 - Rubbed (7)

17 - Nerve (5)

21 - Republic in W Africa (4)

22 - Turning force (6)

23 - One who steers boats (3)

24 - Outlines (8)

25 - Individual (6)

Down

1 - Money pouches (6)

2 - Seized with teeth (6)

3 - Many times (5)

4 - Complete (7)

5 - Inconsistency (8)

6 - Number in soccer team (6)

12 - Cover with ice (8)

14 - Enthusiastic (7)

16 - Writing implement (6)

18 - Expels (6)

19 - Horn (6)

20 - Understand (5)

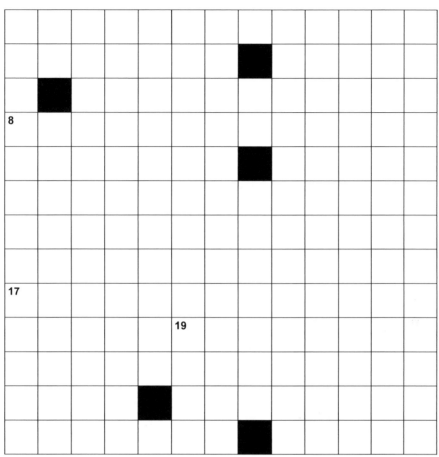

Across

1 - Agreeable sound or tune

4 - Wealthy

7 - Liquid measure

8 - Inhales

9 - Stretched tight (of a muscle)

11 - Unproven

15 - Hamper

17 - Sea duck

19 - Assimilate again

20 - Behaved

21 - Walked upon

22 - Blowing in puffs (of wind)

Down

1 - Capital of Victoria in Australia

2 - Next after sixth

3 - Dispute or competition

4 - Respire with difficulty

5 - Less quiet

6 - Blazes

10 - All people

12 - Massaging

13 - Elongated rectangles

14 - Fable

16 - Liam ___ : Schindler's List actor

18 - Bring on oneself

Across

1 - BRLLNT

6 - BPD

8 - RLC

9 - SWM

10 - MRGN

12 - TRWL

13 - PLM

15 - PCH

16 - SHS

17 - SDSHWS

Down

1 - BBYSTTR

2 - LDY

3 - RBG

4 - TLGRPH

5 - CNMSTS

7 - PSNS

11 - MTHD

14 - LGS

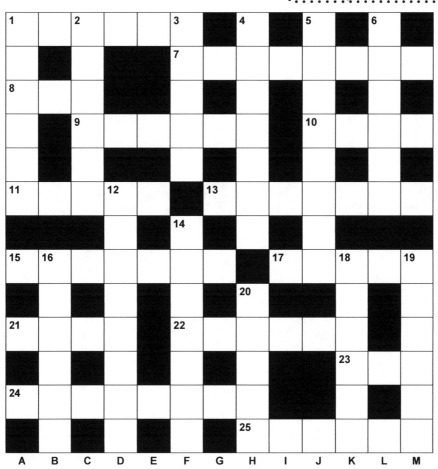

Across

1 - Spiny tree or shrub (6)

7 - Worrying problem (8)

8 - Not well (3)

9 - Opposite of an acid (6)

10 - Fine open fabric (4)

11 - Impertinence (5)

13 - Knight of King Arthur (7)

15 - Mark written under the letter c (7)

17 - Assumed proposition (5)

21 - The south of France (4)

22 - Soothed (6)

23 - Frozen water (3)

24 - Summon to return (4,4)

25 - Symbol or representation (6)

Down

1 - Sour to the taste (6)

2 - Ablaze (6)

3 - In front (5)

4 - Enchanting (7)

5 - Eg rugby or tennis (4,4)

6 - Modern ballroom dance (3-3)

12 - Qualified for entry (8)

14 - Extremely cold (7)

16 - ___ Wood: US actor (6)

18 - Positioned in the middle (6)

19 - Shining (6)

20 - Individual piece of snow (5)

29

28 Word Square

Playthings

Unwrap

Abominable snowman

Cut

29 Word Square

Cuts the grass

Quartz-like gem

Pottery

Turn or slide violently (of a vehicle)

Across

1 - Homeless person (4)

3 - Has to (4)

Down

1 - Computer virus (4)

2 - Touched (4)

A E F I L M
O R S T U W

Across

3 - Talk wildly (4)

4 - Wizard (4)

5 - Roman Emperor (4)

6 - Mischievous god in Norse mythology (4)

7 - Spiritual teacher (4)

Down

1 - Study of lawbreaking (11)

2 - Overly polite (11)

Across

1 - Stage plays (6)

4 - Worshipped (6)

9 - Walked upon (7)

10 - Medical practitioners (7)

11 - Quoted (5)

12 - Rafael ___ : Spanish tennis star (5)

14 - Old-fashioned (5)

15 - Wild dog of Australia (5)

17 - Nadir (anag) (5)

18 - Submarine weapon (7)

20 - Relaxed (7)

21 - Annoying person (6)

22 - Organs that secrete (6)

Down

1 - Disengage (6)

2 - Take up of a practice (8)

3 - Assisted (5)

5 - Move downwards (7)

6 - Repeat (4)

7 - Type of engine (6)

8 - Diligent (11)

13 - Decline in activity (8)

14 - Mournful (7)

15 - Adoring (6)

16 - Classifies; sorts (6)

17 - Lowed (anag) (5)

19 - Kevin ___ : former Australian Prime Minister (4)

A B C D E F G H I J K L M N O P Q R S T U V W X Y Z

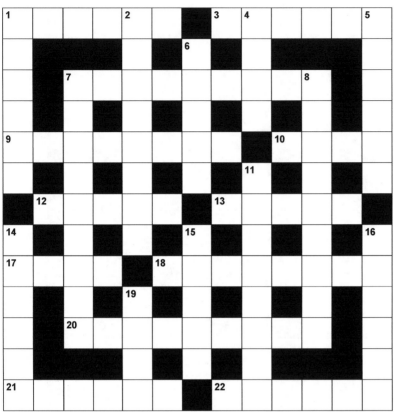

A B C D E F G H I J K L M N O P Q R S T U V W X Y Z

Across

1 - No one (6)

3 - Striped animals (6)

7 - Staying (9)

9 - Compassion (8)

10 - Canine tooth (4)

12 - Links wool together (5)

13 - Crawl (5)

17 - Dispatched (4)

18 - Renounce under oath (8)

20 - Decade from 1970 - 1979 (9)

21 - Parrot sound (6)

22 - Burn (6)

Down

1 - Immature water insects (6)

2 - Control (8)

4 - Depart from (4)

5 - Miserly (6)

6 - Elevators (5)

7 - Cud chewing animals (9)

8 - Inelegant (9)

11 - Having faith in (8)

14 - Incidental remarks; stage whispers (6)

15 - Articulation; shared by two or more (5)

16 - ___ jump: event in athletics (6)

19 - Affirm solemnly (4)

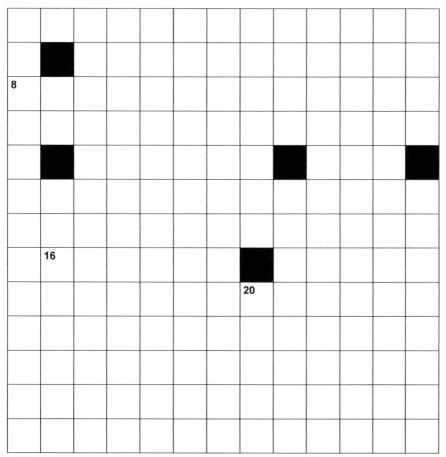

Across

1 - Long mountain chain

7 - Feigns

8 - Grassland

9 - Spinal (anag)

10 - Travel on water

11 - Rushes

13 - Safe places

15 - Report of an event

17 - Dark brown colour

21 - Jar lids

22 - The words of a song

23 - One and one

24 - Bleak; stark

25 - Small finch

Down

1 - Tray

2 - Pass (of time)

3 - Small insect

4 - Restrained

5 - Restore confidence to

6 - Value; respect

12 - Wedge to keep an entrance open

14 - Reveal

16 - Enclosed recess

18 - Points (anag)

19 - Nimble

20 - Type of porridge

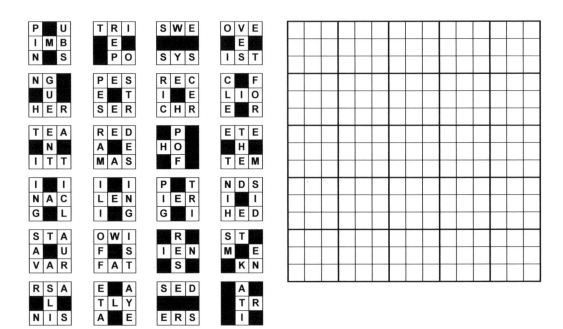

Can you slot the jigsaw pieces into the grid correctly, to create a completed crossword? Use the clues we have listed below to help you out. The grid exhibits standard crossword grid symmetry.

Across

1 - The US flag (5,3,7)

9 - Coated (9)

10 - Show-off (5)

11 - Tortilla topped with cheese (5)

12 - Mercifully (9)

13 - Most saccharine (8)

14 - Made fun of someone (6)

16 - A complex whole (6)

18 - Trinkets (anag) (8)

22 - Very confused situation (9)

23 - One who always puts in a lot of effort (5)

24 - Outstanding (of a debt) (5)

25 - Regained one's strength (9)

26 - Santa Claus (6,9)

Down

1 - Money put aside for the future (7)

2 - Structure resembling an ear (7)

3 - Small mistake in speech (4,2,3,6)

4 - Extreme form of scepticism (8)

5 - Short track for storing trains (6)

6 - Agents (15)

7 - Old Spanish currency (pl) (7)

8 - Moved away from the right course (7)

15 - Confrere (anag) (8)

16 - Incidental result of a larger project (4-3)

17 - Remain alive (7)

19 - Witty saying (7)

20 - Walks with long steps (7)

21 - Religious leader (6)

Across

7 - Avoided (6)

8 - Breathe out (6)

10 - Make amends (7)

11 - Consumed (of food) (5)

12 - Repudiate (4)

13 - Military constructions (5)

17 - ___ Izzard: stand-up comedian (5)

18 - Plant with fronds (4)

22 - Style of Greek architecture (5)

23 - Oval shape (7)

24 - Spirited (6)

25 - Portray (6)

Down

1 - Relies upon (7)

2 - Curbing (7)

3 - Decomposition (5)

4 - Anticipates (7)

5 - Indoor game (5)

6 - Tactical manoeuvre (5)

9 - Placed money in the bank (9)

14 - Instruct (7)

15 - Feeling of hopelessness (7)

16 - Friendly understanding (7)

19 - Enlighten; educate morally (5)

20 - ___ Els: golfing star (5)

21 - ___ DeGeneres: US comedienne (5)

Across

1 - MLESODEMED

5 - RMUUD

7 - AADPN

9 - MLEOYD

10 - TAHU

12 - PSIG

13 - ETAREP

16 - OEDRE

17 - HENSE

18 - OOANRMSCIT

Down

1 - MOEDM

2 - MLADAB

3 - ASSP

4 - ORETNOMME

6 - GINELOSRI

8 - SHA

11 - NOASSE

12 - IPE

14 - TCNOI

15 - GAER

The last letter of each answer will become the first letter of the next answer.
Two other words will appear in the grey diagonals.

1 - Cheeky
2 - Taut
3 - Day of the week
4 - Screaming
5 - Unselfish
6 - Repast
7 - Destiny; fate
8 - Instrument for determining height
9 - Denier (anag)
10 - Small inflatable boat
11 - Servant in a royal household
12 - Food
13 - Female relation
14 - Gives out
15 - Male teacher

40 Word Square

Reduces in length

___ Major: the Great Bear

Russian sovereign

Indian garment

41 Every Letter Counts

1			**2**
3			

A D E H I M
O P S U Y Z

Across

1 - Female domestic helper (4)

3 - Extravagant publicity (4)

Down

1 - Sentimentality (4)

2 - Slumber (4)

42 Ladder Crossword

Across

3 - Wicked (4)

4 - Formal dance (4)

5 - Where a bird lays eggs (4)

6 - Image of a god (4)

7 - Opposite of short (4)

Down

1 - Trustworthy (11)

2 - Act gloomily (anag) (11)

Across

7 - Fame (6)

8 - Large bodies of water (6)

9 - Skilful (4)

10 - Game of chance (8)

11 - Hottest (7)

13 - Perfume (5)

15 - Stomach (5)

16 - Driver of a horse-drawn vehicle (7)

18 - Salve (8)

19 - Rescue (4)

21 - Wonder at (6)

22 - City in NE Italy (6)

Down

1 - ___ Campbell: actress (4)

2 - Very thoughtful (13)

3 - Act of entering (7)

4 - Scoundrel (5)

5 - Railway and road intersection (5,8)

6 - Example (8)

12 - Native of the United States (8)

14 - Prisoner (7)

17 - Removes the skin from (5)

20 - Bad habit (4)

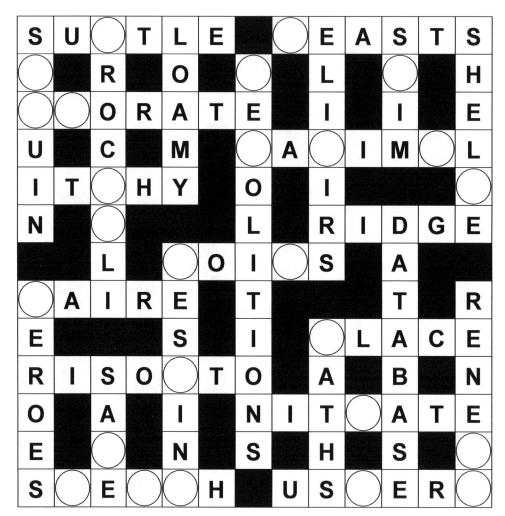

A B C D E F G H I J K L M N O P Q R S T U V W X Y Z

Across

1 - Harasses; hems in (6)

4 - Paler (6)

9 - Mythical bird (7)

10 - Turning forces (7)

11 - Dimensions (5)

12 - Young deer (5)

14 - Utilise (5)

15 - Strongly advised (5)

17 - Stringed instrument (5)

18 - Grotesque monster (7)

20 - Movement of vehicles (7)

21 - Oily (6)

22 - Mixed up or confused (6)

Down

1 - Go around (6)

2 - Dozing (8)

3 - Military vehicles (5)

5 - Distress greatly (7)

6 - Skirt worn by ballerinas (4)

7 - Lifts up (6)

8 - Estimate the value of (11)

13 - Unjustified (8)

14 - Sticks to (7)

15 - Free of an obstruction (6)

16 - Expressed vocally (6)

17 - Plait (5)

19 - Small piece of land (4)

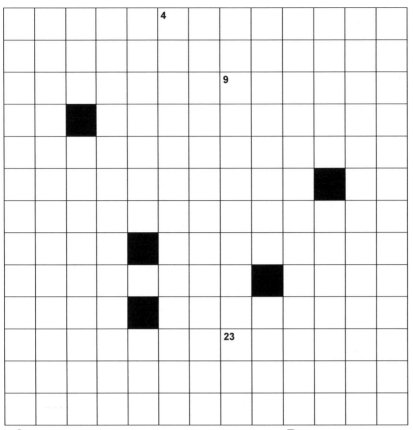

Across

1 - A lament

6 - Smile broadly

8 - Tropical bird

9 - Representation of a person

10 - Not well

11 - Leave out

12 - Make less sensitive

13 - Unfold

15 - Hanging down limply

17 - Make receptive or aware

20 - Bowed stringed instrument

21 - Muhammad ___ : boxing legend

22 - Small village

23 - Obligations

24 - Ruse

25 - Fragrant

Down

2 - Tribal leader

3 - Small heron

4 - Most favourable

5 - Give up

6 - Bison

7 - Standpoint

14 - Normally

15 - Definite; unquestionable

16 - Pointer (anag)

18 - Fishing net

19 - Consumer

20 - Essential

Across

1 - DSVWL

6 - FLK

8 - LMM

9 - NVY

10 - PLSM

12 - TSSL

13 - JSH

15 - LBBY

16 - RCT

17 - NDNGRS

Down

1 - DFNTLY

2 - VW

3 - WLDLY

4 - LMSTN

5 - PRCHTS

7 - DVSBL

11 - PLYD

14 - TRN

45

Across

1 - Drink (6)

5 - Performed an action (3)

7 - ___ Adkins: singer (5)

8 - Ascended (7)

9 - New ___ : Indian capital (5)

10 - Capable of being wrong (8)

12 - Positioned in the middle (6)

14 - Eg monkey or whale (6)

17 - Summon to return (4,4)

18 - Epic poem ascribed to Homer (5)

20 - Mercury alloy (7)

21 - Electronic message (5)

22 - Was in first place (3)

23 - Developed into (6)

Down

2 - Distance travelled (7)

3 - Relating to scripture (8)

4 - Fermented honey and water drink (4)

5 - Speak rhetorically (7)

6 - Anagram of 12 Down (7)

7 - Mix up (5)

11 - Eg rugby or tennis (4,4)

12 - Examination of one's health (7)

13 - Definite; unquestionable (7)

15 - Praise enthusiastically (7)

16 - Inner circle (5)

19 - Transaction (4)

Across

1 - Cook (4)

3 - Auction offers (4)

Down

1 - Suppress (4)

2 - Ventilates; supporters (4)

A B C D E F
H I N R S U

Across

3 - Lead singer of U2 (4)

4 - Dame (anag) (4)

5 - Where a bird lays eggs (4)

6 - A group of three (4)

7 - Killer whale (4)

Down

1 - Feeling of hatred (11)

2 - Not absolute (11)

51 Word Square

Short nail

Fit of shivering

Bend or coil

Brown seaweed

52 Word Square

Chair

Corner

Grows older

Critical examination

48

Across

7 - Give formal consent to (6)

8 - Bestow (6)

10 - Silklike fabric (7)

11 - Enlighten; educate morally (5)

12 - Ran away (4)

13 - Notable achievements (5)

17 - Concentrate on (5)

18 - At a distance (4)

22 - Hard rock (5)

23 - Rise into the air (of an aircraft) (4,3)

24 - Respite (6)

25 - Caress (6)

Down

1 - Please or delight (7)

2 - Manned (7)

3 - Later (5)

4 - Wooded areas (7)

5 - Attach (5)

6 - Becomes worn at the edges (5)

9 - Cautiously (9)

14 - Decade from 1940 to 1949 (7)

15 - Has enough money to pay for (7)

16 - Worked hard (7)

19 - Burning (5)

20 - Satiates (5)

21 - Currently in progress (5)

A B C D E F G H I J K L M N O P Q R S T U V W X Y Z

50

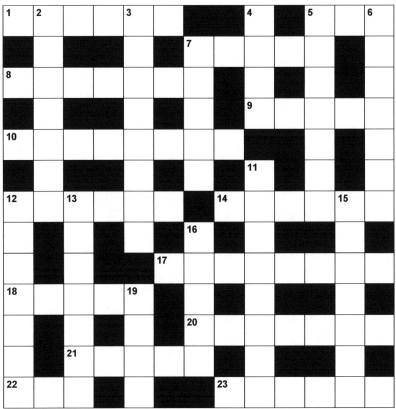

A B C D E F G H I J K L M N O P Q R S T U V W X Y Z

Across

1 - Undid (6)

5 - In what way (3)

7 - Stadium (5)

8 - Servile (7)

9 - U-shaped curve in a river (5)

10 - Misshapen (8)

12 - Adjusting a musical instrument (6)

14 - Jolted (6)

17 - Socially exclusive (8)

18 - Work out (5)

20 - Group of three plays (7)

21 - Baked sweet desserts (5)

22 - However (3)

23 - Believer in God (6)

Down

2 - Flat highland (7)

3 - Person leaving country (8)

4 - Nothing (4)

5 - Sheltered port (7)

6 - Disobedient (7)

7 - Concur (5)

11 - Conquer (8)

12 - Day of the week (7)

13 - Overlook (7)

15 - Flags of office (7)

16 - Narrow openings; lists (anag) (5)

19 - Northern deer (4)

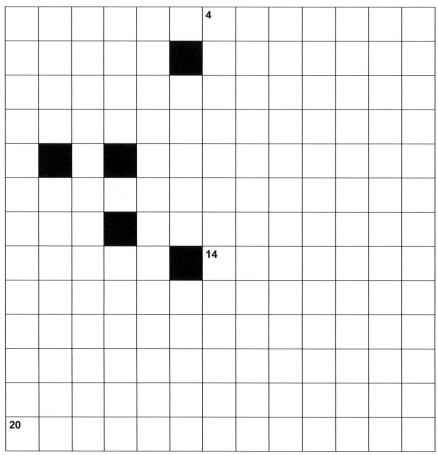

Across

1 - Soft-bodied beetle

5 - Fit of shivering

8 - Living in a city

9 - Caresses with the nose

10 - Alfresco

12 - Wishes for

14 - Wheeled supermarket vehicle

16 - Farm implements

18 - Perform in an exaggerated manner

19 - Opening of a cave

20 - Otherwise

21 - Piece of fabric that covers the head

Down

1 - Adhesive

2 - Paths of electrons around nuclei

3 - Conjecturing

4 - Donors (anag)

6 - Characteristically French

7 - Opposite of westerly

11 - Related to classification

12 - Show to be false

13 - Tools for drilling holes in rocks

14 - African fly

15 - Lapis ___ : blue gemstone

17 - Cook

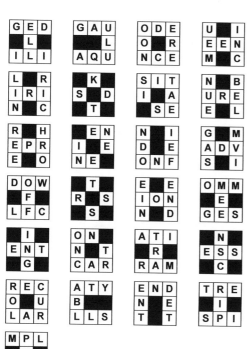

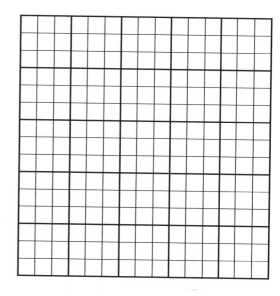

Can you slot the jigsaw pieces into the grid correctly, to create a completed crossword? Use the clues we have listed below to help you out. The grid exhibits standard crossword grid symmetry.

Across

1 - Favourable mention (14)

9 - Biggest (7)

10 - Passenger vehicle (7)

11 - Part of the eye (4)

12 - Severe recession (10)

14 - Estimated (6)

15 - Supplication (8)

17 - Like an eagle (8)

18 - Falls out unintentionally (6)

21 - Explorer (10)

22 - Observed (4)

24 - Take a seat (3,4)

25 - Collapse violently inwards (7)

26 - Belief in one's own ability (4-10)

Down

1 - Turning over and over (7)

2 - What CV stands for (10,5)

3 - Overly submissive (4)

4 - Course of a meal (6)

5 - Remove a monarch (8)

6 - Written copy (10)

7 - Extremely rarely (4,2,1,4,4)

8 - Up-to-date and fashionable (6)

13 - Reprimanding (7-3)

16 - Suggestive remark (8)

17 - Andre ___ : former US tennis player (6)

19 - Genuine (7)

20 - Trust or faith in (6)

23 - Potato (informal) (4)

Across

1 - Grime or dirt (6)

3 - Concealing (6)

7 - Planning to do something (9)

9 - Occurred (8)

10 - Breathe convulsively (4)

12 - Sticks together (5)

13 - Established custom (5)

17 - Large wading bird (4)

18 - Person with a degree (8)

20 - Mexican dip (9)

21 - Waterproof overshoe (6)

22 - Mineral used to make plaster of Paris (6)

Down

1 - South American cowboy (6)

2 - Assembled (8)

4 - Egyptian goddess (4)

5 - Grouchy (6)

6 - Tines (anag) (5)

7 - Urging into action (9)

8 - Be attracted to a person or thing (9)

11 - Printed version of data on a computer (4,4)

14 - Employing (6)

15 - Big (5)

16 - Inert gaseous element (6)

19 - Head coverings (4)

Across

1 - EQIAMURANA

5 - DEPTI

7 - GHIET

9 - CYLLOD

10 - AGTS

12 - EIMT

13 - RCLIOF

16 - ORBTO

17 - IBDUA

18 - IMSMEPHEBR

Down

1 - ETCAZ

2 - SADLEM

3 - DURE

4 - CTBIHNGLU

6 - TLAALAPEB

8 - GTU

11 - RARETD

12 - AMR

14 - MICPH

15 - TBAS

60 Every Letter Counts

Across

1 - Accurate pieces of information (5)

3 - Prod with the elbow (5)

Down

1 - Scowl (5)

2 - Skewer; spear (5)

A C D E F G I K
N O P R S T U W

61 Ladder Crossword

Across

3 - Image of a god (4)

4 - Decapod crustacean (4)

5 - Pitcher (4)

6 - Uncle's wife (4)

7 - Italian acknowledgement (4)

Down

1 - Inconsistency (11)

2 - Act of explaining in detail (11)

Across

1 - Drink greedily (6)

5 - Atmospheric murk; obscure (3)

7 - Bird droppings used as fertiliser (5)

8 - Disturb (7)

9 - Grows weary (5)

10 - Mirth (8)

12 - Stitching (6)

14 - Thick wet mud (6)

17 - Ferdinand ___ : Portuguese navigator (8)

18 - Entrance barriers (5)

20 - Measure of how pressing something is (7)

21 - Period of darkness (5)

22 - Pop music performance (3)

23 - Take into the body (of food) (6)

Down

2 - Improve equipment (7)

3 - Hating (8)

4 - Stick with a hook (4)

5 - Searched for food (7)

6 - Tough animal tissue (7)

7 - Units of heredity (5)

11 - Substance causing a reaction (8)

12 - Method of presenting a play (7)

13 - Squandering (7)

15 - Sideways looks (7)

16 - The entire scale (5)

19 - Wise man (4)

57

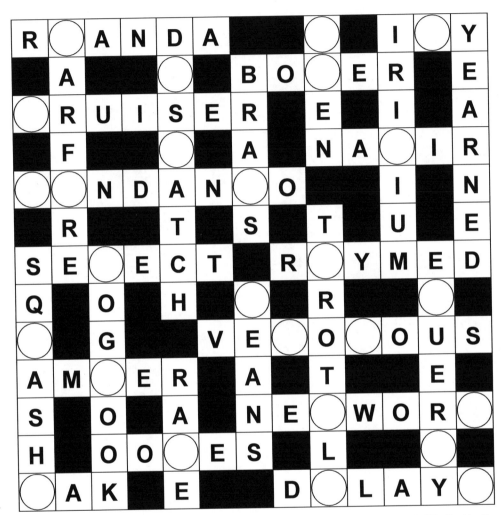

A B C D E F G H I J K L M N O P Q R S T U V W X Y Z

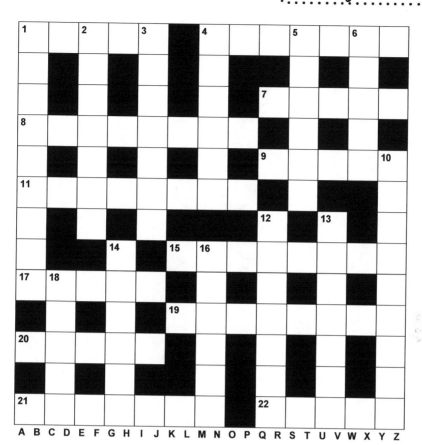

Across

1 - Shy (5)

4 - Temporary stay (7)

7 - Ire (5)

8 - Longevity of an individual (8)

9 - Supplant (5)

11 - Predominate (8)

15 - Being everywhere (8)

17 - Go stealthily or furtively (5)

19 - Umpires (8)

20 - Oven (5)

21 - Horrible (7)

22 - Besmirch (5)

Down

1 - Collections of implements (9)

2 - Anomalies (7)

3 - Flowers with white petals (7)

4 - Jumped up (6)

5 - Female giant (6)

6 - Part of generator (5)

10 - Synthetic fabric (9)

12 - Similar to water (7)

13 - Varied (7)

14 - Flow regulating devices (6)

16 - Windy (6)

18 - Indentation (5)

Across

1 - Repositories

5 - Cereal grain

7 - Leans at an angle

8 - Perceptible to the eye

9 - Crevices

10 - Distribute

12 - Stationary part of a motor

14 - Perceived

17 - Inhales

18 - ___ Robson: British tennis player

20 - Sheikdom in the Persian Gulf

21 - Not tight

22 - Saw (anag)

23 - Lethargic; sleepy

Down

2 - Snobbish

3 - Work surface

4 - Open tart

5 - Diffusion of molecules through a membrane

6 - Wrecked; binned

7 - Stretched tight (of a muscle)

11 - Figure of speech

12 - Swift-flying songbird

13 - Plants that live a year or less

15 - Foes

16 - Biter (anag)

19 - Long nerve fibre

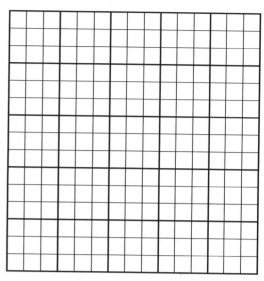

Can you slot the jigsaw pieces into the grid correctly, to create a completed crossword? Use the clues we have listed below to help you out. The grid exhibits standard crossword grid symmetry.

Across

1 - Bovine animals (6)

4 - Of many different kinds (8)

9 - Standard; usual (6)

10 - Evaluator (8)

11 - Long locks of hair (7)

13 - Final stage of a chess match (7)

14 - Defer action (13)

17 - Of mixed character (13)

20 - Large marine flatfish (7)

21 - Edge of a road (7)

23 - Garment worn after a shower (8)

24 - Type of sandwich (6)

25 - Considers in detail (8)

26 - Long thin line or band (6)

Down

1 - War memorial (8)

2 - Submarine weapon (7)

3 - Exposes secret information (5)

5 - Relation by marriage (6-2-3)

6 - In the red (9)

7 - Having a valid will (7)

8 - Moved very quickly (6)

12 - Vulnerable to (11)

15 - Fruit (9)

16 - Starlike symbol (8)

17 - Civilians trained as soldiers (7)

18 - Aperture or hole (7)

19 - Irrational fear (6)

22 - Microscopic fungus (5)

Across

7 - Spiny tree or shrub (6)

8 - Developed into (6)

10 - Extremely cold (7)

11 - Worthy principle or aim (5)

12 - Pleased (4)

13 - Hankered after (5)

17 - Third Greek letter (5)

18 - Every (4)

22 - Speak without preparation (2-3)

23 - Forbidden by law (7)

24 - Was deficient in (6)

25 - Assent or agree to (6)

Down

1 - Luggage (7)

2 - Broken stone used to surface roads (7)

3 - Impersonator (5)

4 - Unit of sound intensity (7)

5 - Name applied to something (5)

6 - Attractive young lady (5)

9 - Extortion by intimidation (9)

14 - Placed a bet (7)

15 - Wrangled over price (7)

16 - Cooled down (7)

19 - Long-handled spoon (5)

20 - Become suddenly understandable (5)

21 - Sudden jerk (5)

The last letter of each answer will become the first letter of the next answer.
Two other words will appear in the grey diagonals.

1 - Stubbornness
2 - Annuals
3 - Building examiner
4 - Saved from punishment
5 - Repudiates
6 - Residential areas
7 - Sat with legs wide apart
8 - ___ & Gabbana: fashion house
9 - Blows up
10 - Theatre worker
11 - Piece of furniture
12 - Repeat something once more
13 - Captive
14 - Official lists or records
15 - Pennant
16 - Take away
17 - Reduce one's expenditure
18 - Strange and mysterious
19 - Jellied ___ : English dish

Domesticated pigs

US state

Female child

Marine flatfish

70 Word Square

Drift in the air

Land measure

At liberty

Adolescent (abbrev)

71 Word Square

Labels

Spots

Bite at persistently

Stitches

Across

1 - Outdo (5)

3 - Is aware of (5)

Down

1 - Opposite of thin (5)

2 - Takes part in a game (5)

A C H I K L M N
O P R S T U W Y

73 Ladder Crossword

Across

3 - Vases (4)

4 - Seal of the Archbishop of York (4)

5 - On top of (4)

6 - Move about aimlessly (4)

7 - US pop star (4)

Down

1 - System of government (11)

2 - Stargazers (11)

65

Across

1 - Flour and water mixture (5)

4 - Spiny egg-laying mammal (7)

7 - Earthy pigment (5)

8 - Careless (8)

9 - New ___ : Indian capital (5)

11 - Type of resistor (8)

15 - To come nearer to (8)

17 - Type of diagram (5)

19 - Mountainous region (8)

20 - Legendary stories (5)

21 - Warming devices (7)

22 - A person's leg (5)

Down

1 - Not acting decisively (9)

2 - Showed a person to their seat (7)

3 - Unfortunate (7)

4 - ___ Cuthbert: Kim Bauer in 24 (6)

5 - Units of linear measure (6)

6 - Compass point (5)

10 - Not in possession of the facts (2,3,4)

12 - Sharp no (anag) (7)

13 - ___ Bedingfield: musician (7)

14 - Eventual outcome (6)

16 - Little bottles (6)

18 - Type of verse (5)

A B C D E F G H I J K L M N O P Q R S T U V W X Y Z

Across

1 - Compartment of a train (8)

5 - Requests (4)

8 - Covered with water (5)

9 - Water bearing rock (7)

10 - Dispossess (7)

12 - Science of matter and energy (7)

14 - Biological catalysts (7)

16 - Domain (7)

18 - Playhouse (7)

19 - Dreadful (5)

20 - Government tax (4)

21 - Amazes (8)

Down

1 - Cover (4)

2 - Actually (6)

3 - Gained through heredity (9)

4 - Organs (6)

6 - Element added to the end of a word (6)

7 - Snakes (8)

11 - Way of plucking violin strings (9)

12 - Put in a pouch (8)

13 - Add (6)

14 - Remains of fire (6)

15 - Small cake-like bread (6)

17 - Expression of regret (4)

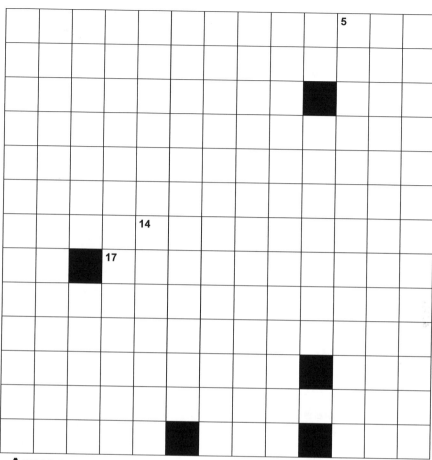

Across

7 - Contemptibly small

8 - Hanging down limply

10 - Ban on publication

11 - Short musical composition

12 - Give up one's rights

13 - Simple

17 - A poison

18 - Outdoor swimming pool

22 - Praise enthusiastically

23 - Hero of the Odyssey

24 - Plant spikes

25 - Lays eggs

Down

1 - Call the validity of a practice into question

2 - Brazilian dance

3 - ___ Balding: TV presenter

4 - Poisonous metallic element

5 - Position or point

6 - Woody tissue

9 - Insatiable

14 - Type of knot

15 - Puzzles composed of many pieces

16 - Be composed of

19 - Tends (anag)

20 - Device for sharpening razors

21 - Slender woman or girl

Across

1 - SSRTMNT

8 - DLR

9 - D

10 - CN

11 - NTN

13 - NST

15 - THM

18 - NRT

19 - RMN

20 - XPLNNG

Down

2 - SLV

3 - GR

4 - TRCS

5 - DCT

6 - TRNMNT

7 - DMNTV

12 - MNTR

14 - SHP

16 - HMN

17 - WRN

Across

7 - Standard; usual (6)

8 - Capital of Canada (6)

10 - Aromatic herb (7)

11 - Small antelope (5)

12 - Require (4)

13 - Academy award (5)

17 - Prod with the elbow (5)

18 - Where darts players throw from (4)

22 - Spring flower (5)

23 - Exceeds; surpasses (7)

24 - Beginner (6)

25 - Extraterrestrial rock (6)

Down

1 - Continuing (7)

2 - Commanded (7)

3 - Maritime (5)

4 - Piece of furniture (7)

5 - Frenzied (5)

6 - Conjuring trick (5)

9 - Roman Catholic prelate (9)

14 - Go faster than (7)

15 - Tenth month of the year (7)

16 - Ascertain dimensions (7)

19 - Natural satellites (5)

20 - Small fruit used for oil (5)

21 - Semiaquatic mammal (5)

Across

7 - EGELI

8 - MOSEO

9 - RTUORIB

10 - EAS

11 - SRVIINCTEDE

14 - LAE

16 - AMILCCU

19 - LREAY

20 - EKELS

Down

1 - BBOL

2 - RRENEA

3 - EIMS

4 - BSEMSO

5 - GOSF

6 - TEDPRA

11 - LDEVUA

12 - ACDYSE

13 - XIEDET

15 - YAWR

17 - KALE

18 - TSAM

Across

1 - Big cat (5)

3 - Exhales air (5)

Down

1 - Pollex (5)

2 - Positions in a hierarchy (5)

A B E G H I K L
M N O R S T U W

82 Ladder Crossword

Across

3 - Travel at speed (4)

4 - Metal fastener (4)

5 - What we hear with (4)

6 - ___ Macpherson: supermodel (4)

7 - Highest adult male singing voice (4)

Down

1 - Award for third place (6,5)

2 - Type of fat (11)

73

Across

1 - Eating a midday meal (8)

5 - Capital of the Ukraine (4)

8 - Send money (5)

9 - Pin tops (anag) (7)

10 - Compels to do something (7)

12 - Imaginary mischievous sprite (7)

14 - Cut pieces off something hard (7)

16 - Part of a gun (7)

18 - Car motors (7)

19 - Excuse of any kind (5)

20 - Abominable snowman (4)

21 - Getting away from (8)

Down

1 - Old Italian currency (pl) (4)

2 - Agile (6)

3 - Young bird (9)

4 - Concept (6)

6 - Cast doubt upon (6)

7 - Disappeared (8)

11 - US state (9)

12 - Shiny; sparkly (8)

13 - Move about restlessly (6)

14 - Serious situation (6)

15 - Type of sandwich (6)

17 - Chinese dynasty (4)

A B C D E F G H I J K L M N O P Q R S T U V W X Y Z

A B C D E F G H I J K L M N O P Q R S T U V W X Y Z

Across

7 - Type of sausage (6)

8 - Tiny fish (6)

9 - Article of clothing (4)

10 - Discern (8)

11 - Overturned (7)

13 - Sea inlet (5)

15 - Healthy skin transplanted (5)

16 - Made the sound of a duck (7)

18 - Bodily exertion (8)

19 - Linear unit (4)

21 - Advance evidence for (6)

22 - First weekday (6)

Down

1 - Father (4)

2 - The fifth period of the Palaeozoic era (13)

3 - Skin eruptions (7)

4 - Shadow (5)

5 - Exclamations such as 'dear me!' (13)

6 - Come together (8)

12 - Bleach (8)

14 - Repositories of antiques (7)

17 - Measured or classified (5)

20 - Converse (4)

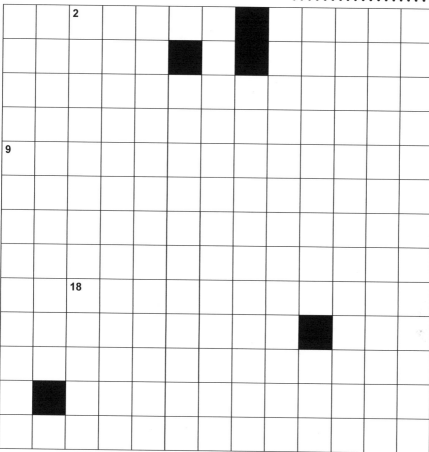

Across

1 - Tennis officials

4 - Light canoe

7 - Motet (anag)

8 - Make less taut

9 - Monetary unit of South Africa

10 - Material from which metal is extracted

11 - Sued (anag)

15 - Sailor of a light vessel

17 - Invalid; void

19 - That vessel

20 - Finish

24 - Give authority to

25 - Hazardous; dangerous

26 - Extinct birds

27 - Contrast

Down

1 - Complete; absolute

2 - Power; strength

3 - Inclined plane

4 - ___ Egan: Westlife singer

5 - Bonds of union

6 - Royal domain

8 - Framework for moving the injured

12 - Very cold

13 - ___ Winehouse: singer

14 - Compete

16 - ___ Bedingfield: musician

18 - Oily organic compound

21 - Recipient of money

22 - Nocturnal birds of prey

23 - Small drink of spirits

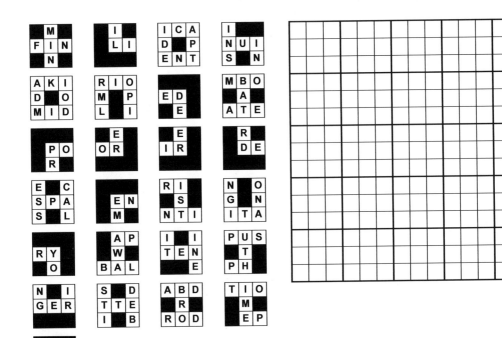

Can you slot the jigsaw pieces into the grid correctly, to create a completed crossword? Use the clues we have listed below to help you out. The grid exhibits standard crossword grid symmetry.

Across

4 - Dissatisfaction; boredom (5)

6 - Items made from fired clay (7)

8 - Failure to fulfil a duty (10)

9 - Musical composition (4)

10 - Gnawing animal like a rat (6)

11 - Statement of commemoration (7)

12 - Given to thievery (5-8)

16 - Relating to knowledge based on deduction (1,6)

17 - With hands on the hips (6)

19 - Spherical object (4)

20 - Overawe (10)

21 - Feeling of hopelessness (7)

22 - Singing voice (5)

Down

1 - Within a space (6)

2 - Hurting; throbbing (8)

3 - Suave; stylish (8)

4 - Involve in conflict (7)

5 - Paint (anag) (5)

6 - Head of the government (5,8)

7 - Period between childhood and adulthood (5)

13 - Lacking intelligence and sense (8)

14 - Hot and humid (8)

15 - Arguer (7)

16 - Prize (5)

17 - Confess to be true (5)

18 - One of the halogens (6)

Across

7 - ___ Keys: US singer (6)

8 - Modern ballroom dance (3-3)

9 - Put down (4)

10 - Electronic message (5)

12 - Ascend (5)

14 - Every (4)

16 - Opposite of low (4)

18 - Camel-like animal (5)

20 - Assumed proposition (5)

22 - Throb; dull pain (4)

25 - Cut down a tree (6)

26 - ___ Wood: US actor (6)

Down

1 - Simple non-flowering plant (4)

2 - Sour to the taste (6)

3 - Water barrier (3)

4 - Highest point (4)

5 - Front of a building (6)

6 - Cup (7)

11 - Clock face (4)

13 - Smile broadly (4)

15 - Dealt with a tough question (7)

17 - Mark ___ : US actor (6)

19 - Spiny tree or shrub (6)

21 - Helper; assistant (4)

23 - Become healthy again (of a wound) (4)

24 - Nourished (3)

Across

1 - Smash (5)

3 - Rounded protuberances on camels (5)

Down

1 - Bungle (5)

2 - Furnaces (5)

A B C E H I K L
M N O P R S T U

90 Ladder Crossword

Across

3 - Rime (anag) (4)

4 - Long periods of history (4)

5 - High fidelity (abbrev) (2-2)

6 - Simple non-flowering plant (4)

7 - British nobleman (4)

Down

1 - Calm and sensible (5-6)

2 - Radically (11)

Across

7 - EHTME

8 - AUCIR

9 - CAUIBVO

10 - IBN

11 - BTNOCOINUAR

14 - BNA

16 - OCSNREF

19 - UINRE

20 - ITRAL

Down

1 - BAST

2 - ENAEVL

3 - UEPR

4 - CAIACA

5 - BCIR

6 - NINNAT

11 - CDIAND

12 - IRCHSE

13 - BAIERI

15 - BLRU

17 - STNE

18 - OSLE

Across

1 - With hands on the hips (6)

3 - Ice shoes (6)

7 - Chunkiness (9)

9 - Excellent (8)

10 - Garment for the foot (4)

12 - Skewered meat (5)

13 - Drenches (5)

17 - ___ Egan: Westlife singer (4)

18 - Small pocket tool (8)

20 - General erudition (9)

21 - Eg Athenians (6)

22 - Uttered (6)

Down

1 - Seek to hurt (6)

2 - Highly critical remark (8)

4 - Capital of the Ukraine (4)

5 - Long-legged wading birds (6)

6 - Sinks (anag) (5)

7 - Officially registered name (9)

8 - Accumulate for future use (9)

11 - Excessively emotional (6,2)

14 - Popular winter sport (6)

15 - Flat-bottomed vessels (5)

16 - Establish by calculation (6)

19 - Snatched (4)

A B C D E F G H I J K L M N O P Q R S T U V W X Y Z

A B C D E F G H I J K L M N O P Q R S T U V W X Y Z

Across

7 - In an absorbing manner (13)

8 - Dependable (8)

9 - Ask questions (4)

10 - Imprisonment (7)

12 - Accolade (5)

14 - Puff on cigarette (5)

16 - Male sibling (7)

19 - Affirm solemnly (4)

20 - Thawed (8)

22 - Lacking complexity (13)

Down

1 - Sheet of paper (4)

2 - Metamorphic rock (6)

3 - Anyone (7)

4 - Spirited horse (5)

5 - Incomparable (6)

6 - Last (8)

11 - Motionless (8)

13 - Movement of vehicles (7)

15 - Show servile deference (6)

17 - Chest (6)

18 - Leaps (5)

21 - Not odd (4)

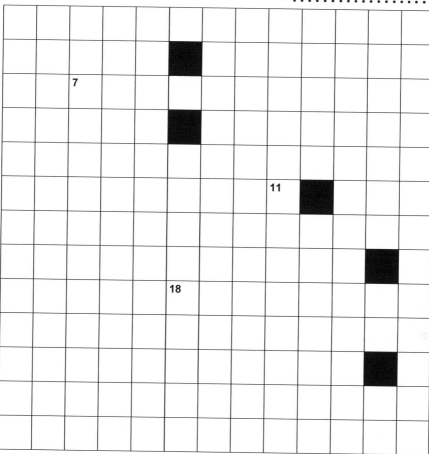

Across

1 - Brandy distilled from cherries

3 - Feeling a continuous dull pain

7 - Halted temporarily

9 - Food of the gods

10 - ___ of Wight: largest island of England

12 - Tool for boring holes

13 - Skewered meat

17 - Not at home

18 - Curved surface of a liquid in a tube

20 - Opposite of lateness

21 - Vitreous

22 - Thoroughfare

Down

1 - US state

2 - Person who buys goods

4 - Give up one's rights

5 - Classifies; sorts

6 - Send money

7 - Conquer; master

8 - Moves away from

11 - Army unit

14 - Seizing

15 - Darken

16 - Feature

19 - Part of the eye

Across

1 - BNDND

8 - BSRVTRY

9 - SCLR

11 - VS

13 - RL

14 - WLNT

16 - CMPSTN

18 - BLLK

Down

2 - BS

3 - NRML

4 - VL

5 - MTN

6 - HPSCTCH

7 - BYZNTN

10 - NM

12 - LMN

15 - YG

17 - NK

Across

1 - Rises (anag) (5)

4 - Having a valid will (7)

7 - Bad-tempered (5)

8 - Private detective (8)

9 - Item of clothing (5)

11 - Showing deep and solemn respect (8)

15 - Large fish (8)

17 - Journeys (5)

19 - Breaking in two (8)

20 - Breathe out loudly when asleep (5)

21 - Chooses (7)

22 - Levies (5)

Down

1 - Written below the line (of text) (9)

2 - Keep for future use (7)

3 - Seafarers (7)

4 - Bird with a long coloured beak (6)

5 - Main tree stems (6)

6 - Relit (anag) (5)

10 - Adolescents (9)

12 - Set of three things (7)

13 - Musical performance (7)

14 - Not dense (6)

16 - Sport Andy Murray plays (6)

18 - Wash with clean water (5)

98 Every Letter Counts

Across

1 - Remove errors from software (5)

3 - Opposite of tall (5)

Down

1 - Curbs (5)

2 - Gleam; glitter (5)

A B D E G H I L
M N O P R S T U

99 Ladder Crossword

Across

3 - Hoodwink (4)

4 - Domesticated (of animals) (4)

5 - Pleased (4)

6 - Long nerve fibre (4)

7 - Frozen rain (4)

Down

1 - The recording of a still image (11)

2 - Extremely (11)

Frozen rain

Breezy

Type of golf club

Medium-sized feline

Solutions

1

```
I N D I A # G R A N D E E
M # E # T # A # A # L # #
P # A # T # U # S T R A Y
A U D I E N C E # U # T #
R # P # N # H # A R M E D
T E A R D R O P # E # E #
I # N # S # D # F # M # #
A # U # E T C E T E R A # A
L E A R N # R # E # R # N
# A # B # H A M P E R E D
G R O A N # C # S # A # I
# L # N # T # E # R # N #
A S P E C T S # A X I N G
```

2

```
S # S # V # # C # B # O
C R E D I T # C O L O U R
R # C # N # P # N # O # D
A N O D Y N E # T A B L E
T # N # L # R # E # Y # R
C O D E # B E A N O # # #
H # S # C # G # T # C # S
# # C H A R M # F O O T #
U # T # O # I # S # R # A
S C R A P # N A T U R A L
E # I # P # E # A # L
R O C K E T # O R A C L E
S # K # R # # T # T # D
```

3

```
D U M P L I N G # E A T S
# P # L # N # R # N # E
O S I E R S # O R G A N S
# C # A # H O W # I # E
F A C T # O # N I N E T Y
# L # R # E
R E V I S E # A B S U R D
# N # Q # A
I G U A N A # J A P E
# E # N # B A A # I # T
S C H E M A # R E F L U X
# K # L # S # I # F # R
D O Z Y # H E A V Y S E T
```

4

```
I S L A N D # S C A M P I
M # E # E # N # A # I # M
P L A C E B O # P # D # A
O # R # D # N E T T I N G
S I N G S # S # U # # E
E # I # # S E # R O L E S
# # N # P I Q U E # I #
C I G A R # U # # S # P
O # # E # I # E N T E R
H A B I T A T # A # E # E
O # Y # E # U R G E N C Y
R # T # N # R # E # E # E
T R E N D S # G R A D E D
```

5

```
S U B T L E T Y # A X E D
# P # R # M # E # S # V #
A G O U T I # A N S W E R
# R # C # N O R # A # N #
H A C K # E # S Q U A S H
# D # E # N # L #
F E R R E T # L A T E S T
# E # U # I #
L O G J A M # L # S I Z E
R # O # E E L # T #
L I A I S E # A F I E L D
# B # N # T # B # L # E #
Z I P S # S P Y G L A S S
```

6

```
# R E J O I N D E R #
S # L # P # E # M # D
T E M P E R A T U R E
A # N # R # L # P
N E T T L E # F A I R
D # R # Y # D # T # E
A X E D # R E N E W S
R # A # T # A # S
D E S T R U C T I V E
S # O # I # O # R # D
# U N B O U N D E D #
```

7

```
M A L I # A # E # I # A # D
N # N O N F L A M M A B L E
K N I T # O # M # P # E # F
I # E # D I S C R E E T L Y
S H O R T E N # A # T # I
I # W # T # S # U N I F Y
L # E X P E R T I S E # E
D A T A # R # I # W I S H
T # V E R D I G R I S # N
S I R E N # I # A # P # N
O # # E # C # T E N A N T S
A N T I M A T T E R # P # E
N # O # I # I # R # E R N E
E N T R E P R E N E U R # C
W # S # S # R # D # S E E M
```

8

```
F # G # I # # D # B # A
I C I C L E # F I L L E D
E # M # I # M # L # A # D
L A M B A D A # E D D I E
D # I # D # C # M # E # D
E A C H # G A M M A
D # K # C # D # A # E # A
# A H E A D # C L A M
A # G # E # M # F # E # A
L I L A C # I L L E G A L
G # E # K # A # A # I # G
A M B L E D # C I C A D A
E # E # D # L # C # M
```

9

```
T U C K
R . . E
A . . Y
P I G S
```

10

```
C . . W
U R G E
L . . S
M U T T
I . . C
N I R O
A . . U
T E E N
I . . T
O M A R
N . . Y
```

11

```
B B C . . B G B
A B O A R D . B Y P L A Y
S N I L A E T
S T U B B L E . N O B L E
O S S T D E S
O B E Y . S T A B S
N S T E Y B B
. B E A R D . B O R E
C I N B A U E
L I B R A . O B L I Q U E
U S B X I U A
B E E T L E . O B J E C T
S N E . . I T H
```

12

```
E . I . B . . E . C . P
M I S H A P . E X U L T S
B O N C P I A
A L L E G R O . A W F U L
R A S N N F M
K I T H . A S I D E
S E P T S J H
. V O C A L . H A L O
G U S N F G
U P S E T . C R O Q U E T
T I M Y X E
S Y N T A X . Z E B R A S
Y G N . . D . S
```

13

```
B . G . S . . R . L . B
E U R O P E . D E D U C E
E . E . I . S . C . N . V
S H A C K L E . I R A T E
W . T . Y . R . T . R . L
A X E D . G I V E N
X . R . S . O . S . A . L
. . B O N U S . A D Z E
E . L . U . S . L . J . A
Q U I F F . L A Y O U T S
U . S . F . Y . R . D . H
I M P E L S . W I G G L E
P . S . E . . . C . E . D
```

14

```
. C H O C K A B L O C K .
D . O . L . S . E . A . A
I . T . E A S E D . P A R
M E D I A . I . G . R . R
I . O . R S . E L I Z A .
N E G L E C T S . . . . N
I . S . D . . R . C . . G
S . . . E S T I M A T E .
H I G H S . T . V . R . M
I . A . A . I M B U E . E
N I B . U N T I E . I . N
G . L . N . O . R . D . T
. R E P A T R I A T E D .
```

15

```
. L . R . G . Q . O . K
M I S U S E . U N L O A D
. M . B . L . I . D . R
J E E R . . . Z E B R A
. . . I . W . . . O . O
. C H A I N . Y A K S .
. V . . I . A . . . E
D E M I . F I V E S
N . G . . . E . N
T R U T H . . . E S P Y
U . A . O . A . E . I
B R O N C O . X E R X E S
E . A . F . E . S . R
```

16

```
B . A . A . . C . C . B
A T T A C K . B E S I D E
N . T . R . C . R . D . S
A M E R I C A . A D E L E
N . M . D . T . M . R . T
A L P S . B A S I S
S . T . C . M . C . C . B
. B Y W A Y . C O V E
B . C . N . R . A . P . E
A L I B I . A F F L I C T
T . G . C . N . I . O . L
C R A V A T . A R O U S E
H . R . L . . . E . S . S
```

17

	C	A	R	A	P	A	C	E	
	L		C		S		G		
T	I	G	H	T		S	T	R	I	P
R		A		S		A		E		E
E	W	E	R		K	I	L	T	E	R
L			S		L				I	
L	A	Y	M	A	N		S	K	E	W
I		E		F		M		N		I
S	A	M	B	A		A	L	O	N	G
		E		R		L		T		
	N	O	I	S	I	E	S	T		

21

S			D
Y	E	T	I
N			S
D	I	S	C
I			U
C	O	W	S
A			S
T	A	X	I
I			O
O	P	E	N
N			S

18

A	K	I	M	B	O	V	E	R
I	S	E	S	T	A	T	E	S
L	I	T	E	D	E	A	L	C
A	D	T	R	A	S	N	Y	R
E	E	X	T	O	I	S	O	A
R	R	E	N	O	L	M	U	W
E	A	I	H	T	O	O	N	L
N	N	S	R	E	T	S	G	A
G	I	S	K	S	I	R	E	Y

19

D	I	L	L
I	D	E	A
L	E	V	Y
L	A	Y	S

20

K	I	N	G
E			A
R			U
B	O	W	L

22

I	N	C	H		S	P	E	C	I	F	I	C
N		H		C		L		L		A		H
D	R	A	C	H	M	A		A	C	C	R	A
E		I		A		I		I		T		R
S	C	R	A	M		C	O	R	P	O	R	A
C				P		E		V		R		C
R	E	C	O	I	L		C	O	R	S	E	T
I		O		O		D		Y			E	
B	A	L	A	N	C	E		A	C	T	O	R
A		O		S		C		N		U		L
B	U	N	C	H		I	N	C	E	N	S	E
L		E		I		D		E		I		S
E	C	L	I	P	S	E	S		A	C	E	S

23

E	N	J	O	Y	S		C		K		E
X		E		P	L	A	N	N	I	N	G
H	O	T		I		D		O		E	
O		S	N	E	E	Z	E		C	U	R	B
R		A		S		N		K		G	
T	E	M	P	O		A	C	R	O	N	Y	M
		L		P		E		U			
T	I	T	A	N	I	C		S	T	A	V	E
	G		T		A		A		L		A
Q	U	A	Y		Z	O	D	I	A	C		R
	A		P		Z		I			O	F	F
I	N	C	U	B	A	T	E		V		U
	A		S		S		U	N	W	E	L	L

24

P	O	N	C	H	O		P		M		E
U		I		F	A	L	L	I	B	L	E
R	A	P		T		E		S		E	
S		P	I	G	E	O	N		M	O	V	E
E		E		N		A		A		E	
S	E	D	G	E		W	R	I	T	I	N	G
		L		Z		Y		C			
S	C	R	A	P	E	D		C	H	E	E	K
R		C		S	G		J		L	
M	A	L	I		T	O	R	Q	U	E		A
Y		A		F		A		C	O	X		O
C	O	N	T	O	U	R	S			T		O
	N		E		L		P	E	R	S	O	N

25

29

M	O	W	S
O	P	A	L
W	A	R	E
S	L	E	W

26

30

27

31

28

T	O	Y	S
O	P	E	N
Y	E	T	I
S	N	I	P

32

33

```
A V O I D S . P A S S E D
G . E . A . J . . . E
H . S T E A D F A S T . L
A . U . P A R . E . U
S U B M E R G E . F L U X
T . T . N . Q . E . E
. O R D E R . Q U I P S
K . A . D . R . A . T
N I C K . B A R I T O N E
I . T . H . Z . N . A
G . S E A W O R T H Y . S
H . . U . R . E . E
T H R I L L . G R I N D S
```

37

```
D . D . D . . E . D . F
E V A D E D . E X H A L E
P . M . C . D . P . R . I
E X P I A T E . E A T E N
N . I . Y . P . C . S . T
D E N Y . F O R T S
S . G . E . S . S . D . E
. . E D D I E . F E R N
E . E . U . T . E . S . T
D O R I C . E L L I P S E
I . N . A . D . L . A . N
F E I S T Y . D E P I C T
Y . E . E . . N . R . E
```

34

```
N O B O D Y . Z E B R A S
Y . O . L . X . . . T
M . R E M A I N I N G . I
P . U . I . F . T . R . N
H U M A N I T Y . F A N G
S . I . A . S . T . C . Y
. K N I T S . C R E E P
A . A . E . J . U . L . T
S E N T . F O R S W E A R
I . T . A . I . T . S . P
D . S E V E N T I E S . L
E . . O . T . N . . L
S Q U A W K . I G N I T E
```

38

```
M E D D L E S O M E . E
O . . . A . A . . O
D U R U M . P A N D A
E . E . B . S . O . S
M E L O D Y . U T A H
. . I . A . S . R
P I G S . R E P E A T
I . I . G . A . M . O
E R O D E . S H E E N
N . A . A . O . I
A S T R O N O M I C
```

35

```
S I E R R A . L . R . A
A . L . P R E T E N D S
L E A . H . A . M . M
V . P L A I N S . S A I L
E . S . D H . S R
R E E D S . R E F U G E S
. . O . U . D . R
A C C O U N T . S E P I A
. L . R . C . G . I . D
T O P S . L Y R I C S . R
S . T . O . U . . T W O
D E S O L A T E . . O . I
. T . P . K . L I N N E T
```

39

```
I M P U D E N T I . I
S N A C K A R M . G
U G H Y E O M A . H
O N I E C E A L . T
R I N I R M N T . H
E D O S T I U I . U
N E I T I R T M . R
E N I E R E T E . S
G N I L L E Y A D
```

36

```
S T A R S A N D S T R I P E S
A . U . L . I . I . E . E . T
V A R N I S H E D . P O S E R
I . P . I . I . R . E . . A
N A C H O . L E N I E N T L Y
G . L . F . I . G . S . A . E
S W E E T E S T . T E A S E D
. . H . M . E . N
S Y S T E M . K N I T T E R S
P . U . T . C . F . A . P . T
I M B R O G L I O . T R I E R
N . S . N . E . R . I . G . I
O W I N G . R E C O V E R E D
F . S . U . I . E . E . A . E
F A T H E R C H R I S T M A S
```

40

```
C U T S
U R S A
T S A R
S A R I
```

41

```
M A I D
U   O
S   Z
H Y P E
```

42

```
R   C
E V I L
S   I
P R O M
O   A
N E S T
S   O
I D O L
B   O
L O N G
E   Y
```

45

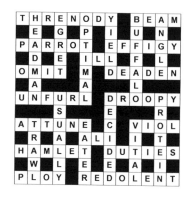

43

46

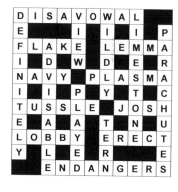

44

47

```
D I S A V O W A L
E   I   I   I   P
F L A K E   L E M M A
I   D W   D   E   A
N A V Y   P L A S M A
I   I   P   Y   T   C
T U S S L E   J O S H
E   A   A   T   N   U
L O B B Y   E R E C T
Y   L   E   R   E
  E N D A N G E R S
```

48

49

C	H	E	F
U			A
R			N
B	I	D	S

50

A			C
B	O	N	O
O			N
M	E	A	D
I			I
N	E	S	T
A			I
T	R	I	O
I			N
O	R	C	A
N			L

51

T	A	C	K
A	G	U	E
C	U	R	L
K	E	L	P

52

S	E	A	T
E	D	G	E
A	G	E	S
T	E	S	T

53

54

55

56

57

```
R E C O M M E N D A T I O N
O   U   E   N   E   R   N   T
L A R G E S T   T R A M C A R
N   K   K   R   H   N   E   E
I R I S   D E P R E S S I O N
N   C   T   E   O   C   N   D
G A U G E D   E N T R E A T Y
  L   L   I   E   I   B
A Q U I L I N E   S P I L L S
G   M   I   N   B   T   U   I
A D V E N T U R E R   S E E N
S   I   G   E   L   S   M   C
S I T D O W N   I M P L O D E
I   A   F   D   E   U   O   R
  S E L F C O N F I D E N C E
```

61

```
D       E
I D O L
S       A
C R A B
R       O
E W E R
P       A
A U N T
N       I
C I A O N
Y       N
```

58

```
G R U N G E   H I D I N G
A   A   I   S       R
U   I N T E N D I N G   U
C   M   H   S   S   R   M
H A P P E N E D   G A S P
O   E   R   T   H   V   Y
  G L U E S   H A B I T
H   L   D   G   R   T   H
I B I S   G R A D U A T E
R   N   H   E   C   T   L
  G U A C A M O L E   I
N   T   T   P       U
G A L O S H   G Y P S U M
```

62

```
G U Z Z L E   G   F O G
  P   O   G U A N O   R
A G I T A T E   F   R   I
  R   T   N   F L A G S   T
L A U G H T E R   G   E   L
  D   I   S   A   E
S E W I N G   S L U D G E
T   A   G   G   L   L
A   S   M A G E L L A N
G A T E S   M   R   N
I   I   A   U R G E N C Y
N   N I G H T   E   E
G I G   E   I N G E S T
```

59

```
A Q U A M A R I N E
Z   E   U   I
T E P I D   E I G H T
E   A   A   D   H   U
C O L D L Y   S T A G
    A   S   T   C
M I T E   F R O L I C
A   A   S   A   U   H
R O B O T   D U B A I
    L   A   E       M
M E M B E R S H I P
```

63

```
R W A N D A   O   I V Y
  A       I   B O X E R   E
C R U I S E R   E   I   A
  F   P   A   N A D I R   N
F A N D A N G O   I   U   E
  R   T   S   T   U
S E L E C T   R H Y M E D
Q   O   H   J   R   Q
U   G   V E N O M O U S
A M B E R   A   T   E
S   O   A   N E T W O R K
H   O O Z E S   L   R
Y A K   E   D E L A Y S
```

60

```
F A C T S
R       P
O       I
W       K
N U D G E
```

64

```
T I M I D   S O J O U R N
O   I   A   P   G   O
O   S   I   R   W R A T H
L I F E S P A N   E   O
B   I   I   N   U S U R P
O U T W E I G H   S   O
X   S   S   A   D   L
E   V   U B I Q U I T Y
S N E A K   R   U   V   E
  O   L   R E F E R E E S
S T O V E   E   O   R   T
  C   E   Z   U   S   E
G H A S T L Y   S M E A R
```

65

66

67

68

69

H	O	G	S
O	H	I	O
G	I	R	L
S	O	L	E

70

W	A	F	T
A	C	R	E
F	R	E	E
T	E	E	N

71

T	A	G	S
A	C	N	E
G	N	A	W
S	E	W	S

72

T	R	U	M	P
H				L
I				A
C				Y
K	N	O	W	S

73

74

75

76

77

78

79

80

81

```
T I G E R
H       A
U       N
M       K
B L O W S
```

82

```
B       C
R U S H
O       O
N A I L
Z       E
E A R S
M       T
E L L E
D       R
A L T O
L       L
```

85

86

83

87

84

88

100

89

B	R	E	A	K
O				I
T				L
C				N
H	U	M	P	S

93

90

94

91

95

92

96

97

98

D	E	B	U	G
A				L
M				I
P				N
S	H	O	R	T

99

P			E
H	O	A	X
O			C
T	A	M	E
O			E
G	L	A	D
R			I
A	X	O	N
P			G
H	A	I	L
Y			Y

100

H	A	I	L
A	I	R	Y
I	R	O	N
L	Y	N	X

47914886R00058

Made in the USA
Lexington, KY
16 December 2015